EROTIC RECIPES

THE TAIWANESE
MODERN LITERATURE SERIES
Edited by Dominic Cheung

*Supported by a matching grant from
the Council for Cultural Affairs in Taiwan*

Drifting Dominic Cheung (Chang Ts'o)

*Erotic Recipes: A Complete Menu for Male
Potency Enhancement* Jiao Tong

Forthcoming

The Mysterious Hualien Chen I-chih

Jiao Tong

EROTIC RECIPES

A Complete Menu
for Male Potency Enhancement

*Translated from the Chinese
by Shao-yi Sun*

GREEN INTEGER
KØBENHAVN & LOS ANGELES
2000

GREEN INTEGER BOOKS
Edited by Per Bregne
København/Los Angeles

Distributed in the United States by Consortium Book
Sales and Distribution, 1045 Westgate Drive, Suite 90
Saint Paul, Minnesota 55114-1065

(323) 857-1115/http://www.greeninteger.com

First Green Integer Edition 2000
©2000 by Jiao Tong
English language translation ©2000 by Shao-yi Sun
Back cover copy ©2000 by Green Integer

Design: Per Bregne
Typography: Guy Bennett
Cover: Photograph of Jiao Tong

Publication of this book was made possible, in part,
through a grant from the Council for Cultural Affairs,
Executive Yuan, Taiwan, R.O.C.

LIBRARY OF CONGRESS CATALOGING IN PUBLICATION DATA
Jiao Tong (Yeh Chen-fu)
Erotic Recipes: A Complete Menu for Male Potency Enhancement
ISBN: 1-892295-84-9
p. cm — Green Integer 101
I. Title II. Series

Contents

MENU C

Preface

As a professional poet and an avid reader of poetry, I have often been frustrated by the experience of reading an anthology in translation, in which the appreciation of poems is totally dissociated from the recognition of poets. On the other hand, reading an anthology of Asian poetry, Western readers tend to focus on the content of the poems more than on the unfamiliar names of the poets. Occasionally, an editor or a translator may attach brief historical accounts or short biographies, but the logical effect of connecting poems to hard-to-remember foreign names is still lacking. Furthermore, an anthology often falls short of presenting the spectrum of poetic variants within a poet's work.

As a solution to the above dilemma, I proposed to the Council for Cultural Affairs in Taiwan to translate a series of five individual volumes of poetry in Chinese, namely, poetry selections from modern Taiwanese poets (Chinese surnames first) Chang Ts'o, Hsi Muren, Chen Yi-chih, Jiao Tong, and Hsu Hui-chih. The above list represents two generations of poets who play an active role in the making of modern Chinese poetry in Taiwan in the past two decades.

Serving as the chief editor of the above series, and with the help of the associate editor Jiao Tong, I have collected poems from the respective poets, and in turn assigned them to qualified translators. I went through each translated poem carefully and consulted with the translators whenever doubts arose. Thus I should be held solely responsible for any textual negligence and translation errors.

— DOMINIC CHEUNG
University of Southern California

About the Poet

Born in K'aohsiung, Taiwan, in 1956, Jiao Tong, penname of Yeh Chen-fu, received his BA and MA in drama from the Chinese Culture University. A poet and essayist, Jiao Tong is now the Executive Deputy Director of the literary supplement of Taiwan's *China Times* and an adjunct lecturer of the Chinese Department at the National Central University. Since 1983, Jiao Tong has published or edited eight poem collections and twelve essay collections. His 1998 poem collection, *A Passage to the City: Selected Poems of Jiao Tong*, has been translated into English.

Introduction

The bond between food and sex has remained constant throughout Chinese history. Confucians, while stressing the overwhelming importance of morality, acknowledged that "eating food and having sex is human nature." Taoists, carefree and fun loving by nature, viewed sex essentially as a special form of food that could help to prolong one's life. Based on the yin-yang theory, the so-called "art of the bedchamber" (fang chung shu) teaches how a man/woman can "absorb sexual energy" (ts'ai pu) from his/her partner so as to achieve longevity. *The Classic of Su Nu* (Su Nu Ching), for example, quotes P'eng Tsu, a legendary figure in Taoist literature who has lived 700 or 800 years, as saying that men and women need to practice the "tao of intercourse" (the art of the yin-yang union) frequently and faithfully in order to attain longevity. If one were to abstain from intercourse, he/she would lose the opportunity to "absorb sexual energy" from the opposite sex and would subsequently die at an early age due to the imbalance of yin and yang. The vocabulary of the "art of the bedchamber," such as "drink" (he), "consume" (shih), and "inhale" (hsi), suggests that, like food, sex is both nourishing and beneficial to health. Although some of the Chinese sexual classics do not necessarily encourage male partners to take medicine or eat "nutritious" food while engaging in intercourse, throughout its long history China has probably developed the most sophisticated and complete menu in the world for enhancing male potency. Food is medicine; medicine is food, as long as they are good for the body. In a male-dominated society, "what is good for the body," either food or medicine or both, is often translated into "magic bullets" that could help men possess/re-possess women.

On the surface, Jiao Tong's poem collection *Erotic Recipes* is a masterful continuation of the world's oldest and most advanced tradition that diffuses the boundary between food and sex. Most ingredients of the recipes, such as tiger penis, shark's fins, prawns, sea cucumbers, Tuckahoe roots, and Peony roots, are traditionally associated with "male potency enhancement" (chuang yang). The marriage between food and literature, on the other hand, is by no means alien in Chinese literary tradition. For some poets and writers, nothing is more inspirational than a course of some great delicacy or a glass of wine. Poetic lines are usually preceded by a feast of rare delicacies, and food and wine become the object of poetic imagination. The great T'ang poet Li Po wrote numerous poems that are laden with overflowing sentiments toward wine drinking. "My Heaven-endowed talents must have their use;/ Throw away a thousand gold coins, and they will all return./Roast the sheep, slaughter the ox! Let's take our pleasure,/and with one long drink, empty three hundred cups!" These lines from "Wine Will Be Served" (chiang chin chiu) still enjoy their enduring power in the Chinese mind of today.

What sets Jiao Tong's collection apart from the traditional bond of sex, food, and literature, however, lies in the fact that, while speaking the vocabulary of the patriarchal on the surface, it actually disturbs or even subverts the patriarchal symbolic through the unraveling of man's primary fear of being deprived of phallic power. If Freudian "castration complex" is evoked by the disturbing realization of woman's "lack" of the penis, then the "impotence anxiety," deeply rooted in the unconscious of modern manhood, is a symptom that is fearful of losing what a man has already had as well as the power associated with it. In a phallocentric society, "an erect pillar" signifies man's ultimate power to penetrate, possess, and investigate the very "mystery" of the woman, and the failure to achieve an "erection," in both real and symbolic sense, means the loss of control over the woman. Modern man's attempt to project a perpetual youth, either through the "erotic recipes" or through the "magic bullet" of Viagra, reflects his determination to gain woman's subjugation and to solidify the very foundation of a male-dominated civilization. In pushing the "chuang yang" (male potency enhancement) fantasy to the level of obsession, Jiao Tong actually brings to light the male hysteria, usually hidden in the dark, toward the female other. On the one hand, the female body, like "raging flame," "unceasingly tantalizes" the male desire ("Flirting with Flowers and Willows"). "With an expectation of three-million years ago," he gets more and more impatient. "Matchlessly hard and firm in surface," he "thirst[s] to touch [her] gentle grassland" and to "enter into [her] roaring lake" ("I Will Rise Again"). But on the other hand, the lustfully pursued woman occupies in patriarchal culture as a threat that disturbs the system and order. The ying force could arouse the male lust, but it could also put out the flaming yang. In order to retain his authority and avoid being overcome by the female other, therefore, men need to continue to produce erections and to try every means to prolong the erection. Jiao Tong's *Erotic Recipes*, if read from this perspective, is an uncanny attempt to unmask the modern man's utmost fear in the post-feminist era.

If Jiao Tong's unmasking of the patriarchal myth has its universal significance, then his experimental endeavor also aims to ridicule the political myth on a local level. Since the Nationalist Government retreated to the island of Taiwan in 1949, the political fantasy of recovering the "lost" mainland has dominated the arena of Taiwan politics. Like an impotent man eager to "rise again," the Nationalists, led by the patriarchal figure Chiang Kai-shek, never ceased to look for the opportunity to regain the mainland "emasculated" by the Communists. By interweaving political slogans like "Self Strengthening in Solemn Respect" and "Never Forget the Days in Chu" with everyday recipes, the poet skillfully undermines the political credibility of the Nationalist Government. The trivialization of the "solemnness" of the Nationalists' political agenda gives the poem collection a carnivalistic feature that is both subversive and comical. To the poet, sex and politics are the two sides of the same coin. Whereas the search for the instant cure for impotence reveals men's innermost feeling of insecurity, the loudly broadcasted propaganda to regain the control of the "lost" mainland is only a twisted reflection of the political impotence of the Nationalist Government.

The Chinese sage will rule a country "like cooking a small fish." Perhaps revolutionary changes do start from the kitchen. The "real" cure for impotence, either sexual or political, therefore, is probably to order a glass of Mexican Tequila or a dish of "Three-Inch Golden Lotus" and then indulge himself in the nostalgic remembering of the days when he was still a "dragon from the north sea" or a "fierce tiger from the south mountain." By doing so he can at least pique his troubled libido or fire his desire in sweet imagination.

—S.Y.S

Ingredients

Mexican Tequila, orange juice, red pomegranate syrup, ice cubes, cherry.

Method

1) Put ice cubes into wineglass, pour Tequila, and then pour in orange juice until 80% full.
2) Place a stirring spoon on the inside edge of the glass, slowly pour red pomegranate syrup into the spoon, and then let syrup naturally saturate to the bottom of the glass.
3) Shake glass lightly until the bottom shows seductive blush.
4) Choose a scarlet cherry to decorate.

Illustration

Slowly pour in red pomegranate syrup and lightly shake wineglass. Visually, be sure to let color produce the leveled effect of "the red banners billow in the west wind."*

This drink is like the nation's liberator who saves the spirit from sickness. It is especially good for situations like political struggle and social intercourse. On the surface, it appears calm and cold, but it will make one feel coquettish after being consumed. On the one hand, it will bring about earthshaking ambition. On the other hand, it will enhance the softness of one's spine as well as the elasticity of one's back muscle, which enables one to bend at a large angle at all times and immediately recover his unmatchable hardness after the action.

This is a drink that arouses one's carnal desire. Driven by desire and thirst, it summons a five-thousand-year-long carnal desire and moral tradition. To achieve a better result, it is recommended one recite Mao Tse-tung's "Snow: To the Melody of *Ch'in Yuan Ch'un.*" After one drinks this, a feeling of broadness and vastness will arise under the belly

* A line from Mao Tse-tung's poem "Mount Liu P'an: To the Melody of *Ch'ing P'ing Yueh.*"

button. Energized with great ambitions, one looks down on ancient heroes and rulers and wants to "challenge heaven with [his] height(s)."* In his eyes, everything appears exceptionally coquettish and charming.

Can it be that the soul kissed in previous life
Comes back searching for lips in this life?
I want to use the tip of my tongue
To taste this sweetness,
This bitterness of remembering,
Oh, this crazy sourness;

I want to use the tip of my tongue
To embrace you until dawn,
Your breasts are crystal champagne glasses,
In the place fondled by the rising sun, red
Is launching a riot against yellow;
That sour subversion on the bottom is making
The density of a romantic revolution.

* The original lines read: "The mountains are dancing silver serpents/And hills, like waxen elephants, plod on the plain,/Challenging heaven with their heights."

Desire is my thought,
A powerful army, guarding
My ambition,
Desires to rest on you, breathing
The flowerbed on your breasts, listening to the
Wild heart beating,
Like the scorching sun, dominating the
Territory of hyperemia.

Can it be that the soul kissed in previous life
Comes back searching for lips in this life?
The lips that long to speak
There left deep traces of a kiss
On the wineglass of fate.

Ingredients

Large shark's fins, home-grown chicken, pig's feet, ox bones, ham, Shaohsin wine, green onion, ginger.

Method

1) First soak the shark's fins: wash clean and dry shark's fins, put them in a big pot full of cold water, and make certain that the water submerges each fin. The next day, dump the fishy water, add 70% full cold water, Shaohsin wine and ginger slices, and cook over high heat until boiling. Simmer for a while and turn off heat. After it turns cold, dump the fishy water and ginger slices. Again add 70% full fresh and cold water, Shaohsin wine, and ginger slices. Repeat the previous procedure: cook over high heat until boiling, turn off heat, and dump the fishy water and ginger slices when cold. Once again add 70% full fresh and cold

water, Shaohsin wine, and ginger slices. Repeat the previous procedures: turn off heat after boiling. When cold, pat dry the rinsed fins and carefully pick out the impure elements.

2) Make soup-stock: one home-grown chicken, a pig's foot, an ox bone, and one segment of ham. Dip into boiled water and rinse. Put into a big pot and add water enough to submerge the four items. Cook over high heat until boiling. Add Shaohsin wine, ginger slices, and a few green onions. Simmer for an hour. Take out green onion and ginger and filter impure elements.

3) Carefully put dry rinsed fins into the pot.

4) Slowly pour soup-stock into the pot up to 70% full.

5) Simmer for six hours.

6) You may add a few drops of red vinegar when serving.

Illustration

It is very time-consuming and labor intensive to cook this dish. Making shark's fins is enjoyable even during the time of execution; one must be brave enough to discard impure elements and display one's national spirit in punishing Han traitors. When cooking, one should behave as if engaging in a revolutionary struggle. Calmly observe the changes and remain unshakable and become even firmer as time goes by. Only by so doing can one draw lessons from the process and reach the realm of becoming more unyielding in adverse circumstances.

A spoon of hot vinegar pours on one's heart,
The sour taste of love
Drips on the scars of history, as if
War has kissed the thickly honeyed Republic —

Light heat slowly simmers out the memory of food,
In a little while, the fragrant breath of sound sleep
Unfastened like buttons,
Don't open lips too easily, don't
Don't expose the tip of the tongue, once
Mouth, mouth opens
They will twine with each other. As if

Counterattack and resurgence
Madly make love —
Opened lips in quiver
Embrace the extended tongue,
Only when the tongue has been through the
changes of life
Can the body be imbued with
Inspiration, we
Draw lessons, we
Gather for joy, like *fin-de-siècle* prosperity,
Hundreds of tastes mix in nakedness, mutually
Valued, depending on each other's
Orgasm.

NEVER FORGET THE DAYS IN CHU*

Ingredients

U.S. choice short ribs, red wine, butter, garlic salt, orange, and lettuce.

Method

1) Cut U.S. choice short ribs into pieces; use the Chateau Ausone Winery Vintage 1971** red wine to soak U.S. choice short ribs overnight.
2) When pan is hot, grease it with butter. Fry U.S. choice short ribs over high heat until the outside becomes slightly crisp. Immediately change to gentle heat and continue to fry. Pour in the red wine used in soaking.

---

* Chu was a small Chinese feudal state in the Western Chou dynasty (1027 BC–770 BC). The capital of the state was originally established in Chi-Chin (today's Chiao-Chou city of Shantung province), but during the Spring and Autumn period (770 BC–480 BC), a time when China's feudal states battled with each other for the dominance of the country, the capital was forced to move to a southern place called Chu. "Never Forget the Days in

3) Extract juice from orange and spread juice on u.s. choice short ribs.
4) When orange juice is about to evaporate, add garlic salt.
5) Before placing u.s. choice short ribs on a plate, use lettuce to cover the bottom.

Note

Try one's best to avoid making this dish when depressed and sorrowful. Avoid by all means shedding tears when putting in u.s. choice short ribs, because tears will change the component of food and lead to dangerous chemical changes.

Illustration

Before frying u.s. choice short ribs, one does not need to wait for the complete evaporation of mois-

---

Chu" was a political slogan of the Nationalist Government after it lost the control of the mainland. Chiang Kai-shek wanted to use Taiwan as a political and military base to recover the lost mainland.
** An allusion to Taiwan's loss of the offIcial seat at the United Nations in 1971.

ture. When cream is put in, water balls will dance on the pan.

As for the texture and quality of u.s. choice short ribs, one must select straight and elastic ones. After chopped into pieces, each should carry a bone in the middle, which looks like the slab on the Taiwu Mountain of Kimmen. When making this dish, one should be full of patience in waiting: avoid no frying pain, fear no hardship, and uphold the spirit of "Never Forget the Days in Chu."

u.s. choice short ribs must be soaked one day before frying. At nightfall, one should take a shower, read sutras, pray, and then sleep in calmness.

The priority of meat lies in its form of expression. The purpose of soaking beef short ribs in wine is to use the fragrance of wine to awaken beef short ribs as well as to awaken some kind of remote memory.

Like a hot slice inserted into the
Buttery legend, we
Fry and embrace each other
Burning hot blood, hungry lips,

27

Our body temperature
Rises in times of love and hate,
As if the spring coldness awakens a hot summer,
The hot summer is waiting for another hot summer.

As if fingers skillful at flirtation, waiting for the
Gradually softened body.
Trembling under me
Exciting flame,
Hug me tightly, if you fear,
In light sour citrus, like first love,
Fermenting in memory, like
Gasping at the border of dreams, like
Raving on sleeping pillows.

SELF STRENGTHENING IN SOLEMN RESPECT*

Ingredients

Sea horses, small cuttlefish, garlic, old ginger, red pepper, Chinese basil, green onion, sugar, Shaohsin wine, soy sauce, and sesame oil.

Method

1) Treat all ingredients as a string of incantation and chant once.
2) Get rid of internal organs of the sea horses and cuttlefish, then wash clean.
3) Peel garlic and cut old ginger into pieces. Cut red pepper into oblique slices and green

---

* One of the two political slogans propagated by the Nationalist Government after the United States severed formal diplomatic relations with Taiwan in 1979. President Nixon paid an official visit to Peking in February 1972 and the Shanghai Communique was signed five months later, which paved the way for the United States to establish full formal diplomatic relations with the People's Republic of China in place of Taiwan (Republic of China) in 1979. Another slogan was "Stay Calm in Adverse Circumstances."

onion into segments. Wash clean Chinese basil and get rid of overgrown stems.

4) Use sesame oil to fry out the mixed flavor of ginger, garlic, pepper, and green onion. Add sea horses, cuttlefish, soy sauce, sugar, and fry thoroughly. Sprinkle Shaohsin wine.

5) Boil until soy sauce is about to evaporate and add Chinese basil. Stir-fry thoroughly.

Note

For Han Chinese, eating sea horses will cause hypertrophy of the prostate. Consequently, they should not try it.

Illustration

The sea horse is accustomed to a single mate. Therefore, its reproduction rate is very low, which brings about the spirit of male potency enhancement and exemplifies the old saying, "When a thing is scarce, it is precious."

A first-class revival base* demands first-class ser-

* The "revival base" refers to the island of Taiwan.

vicemen and civilians, and first-class servicemen
and civilians demand first-class food. This dish
nourishes the essential *chi*, not only capable of over-
coming the physical weakness of servicemen and
civilians but also capable of soothing the spirit of
the country.

For several decades, the policy of appeasement has
spread all over the international community. During the time of life and death, Taiwan has been firm
and determined all along, upholding the faith of
self strengthening and staying calm in adverse circumstances. In forty years, it has quickly wiped out
four kinds of sea horses along the ocean: K'uta sea
horse in Ch'engkung of Taitung, Chi sea horse in
Tungkang, Ch'angchi sea horse and Sanpan sea
horse in Kaohsiung. Later on, Taiwan imports 4.4
million sea horses every year, only second to mainland China in number. Dr. Wilson of McGill University in Canada discovered this secret and has
alarmed the world about the incoming yellow peril.
However

The gland is an ark in turbulent times,
So long as that ark grows slightly longer

Bigger, and harder,
When facing the vast flood
 It turns to a double bed.

That is a secret from deep sea,
The burning sun and trade wind,
Sea horses and cuttlefish,
When the two bodies twine together, that is
A long fishing line, dipping into
The deepest privacy.

Silently blossom like the pearl oyster,
The two bodies twine together,
With no voice, yet still able to
Communicate. Two lips,
Two dry and thirsty lips
Moistened because of the encounter after a long
separation,
Kiss in excitement, tasting
The bitterness of carnival and loneliness, hugging
By a warm fire,
Fire guards the body temperature of memory,
Because memory is our last and
Hardest base.

STRENGTHENING THE BASE*

Ingredients

Black sesame oil, Taiwanese home-grown chicken, old ginger, rice wine, garlic salt, rice.

Method

1) Wash and clean the home-grown chicken, chop it into pieces, quick boil the chopped chicken.
2) Pour black sesame oil into a preheated pot.
3) Slice old ginger, fry the slices in the boiling sesame oil until fragrant, then put chopped chicken in the pot, slightly saute. Turn off gas.
4) Wash and dry rice. Add some rice wine, water, and garlic salt; add sauteed sesame oil and chicken, cook until ready to serve.

---

* Again, the "base" refers to the island of Taiwan, seen by the Nationalists as the foundation to regain the control of the mainland.

Illustration

This dish requires a special ambience when served. You may play marching songs as background music during eating.

The nutritious sesame oil chicken rice can easily increase the density of blood cholesterol. Its tastefulness may easily defeat your control of the diet you've worked so hard at. Every time I make this dish, my weight always increases one to two kilograms. This dish was developed by my mother. She uses it to show love toward her fatherless children. It constantly evokes human stories in memory, and gradually develops its alluring beauty —

You are an empty bowl,
Imbued with the black sesame oil of desire,
Amorously hot
Heating up
Waiting for the spread chopsticks —

Because of you, doors and windows
Have longing,
Longing for breeze passing,
Bring your blowing breath,

Oh, it is the source to strengthen my base,
My disaster;

Because of you, lips
Have emotion.
When I hold my breath,
Your flavor intrudes like wave,
Stirs my longing.

Even if there is a pot of angry hot oil splashing
Burning my face, I am willing to
Taste happiness in pain, only to obtain
Your flavor.

Ingredients

Upstream-going minnows from the Fenghua County of China,* shredded ginger, turtle-snake wine, water from the Athabasca Glacier of Canada, thick soy sauce of Taiwan.

Method

1) Making fish soup is analogous to the revolutionary mission of saving the poor and miserable. One should accurately master the relationship between time and space. Rise at the right moment, push in when opportunity allows, endure what other people cannot bear, and decide what other people cannot resolve.

2) With reverence, wash off the bloody smell of fish and chant "Streams in the Deserts."

3) Put shredded ginger into the Athabasca Gla-

---

* Chiang Kai-shek's birthplace. Chiang was born in the Fenghua County of Chekiang Province in 1887.

cier water. When boiling, let minnows swim nakedly into the water, as if to let them bath in sunshine and happiness.

4) When fish is done, add salt and a few drops of turtle-snake wine.

5) Scoop up fish and, on a plate, arrange disorganized fish in an orderly manner. Take dips in the thick soy sauce of Taiwan when serving.

Illustration

Taiwanese thick soy sauce is a mix of the five flavors. That taste regards the mission of rejuvenating national culture and recovering the lost mainland as its own duty. Its sweetness is mixed up with mild salty and puckery flavors as well as a clear taste of sourness. This sauce is most suitable for Fenghua County's minnows. Be aware that, when eating the fish, one should adopt the non-attached attitude of a traveler and take out the fish after a single dip. Otherwise it will taste sticky.

Originally there were six main glaciers in the Columbia ice field. The Athabasca Glacier is not the longest and largest one. For instance, the neighboring Saskatchewan Glacier is two times the size of the Athabasca Glacier. But the shape of the Athabasca Glacier is the most magnificent. From the bird's-eye view, it looks exactly like a mighty and powerful phallus.

According to a survey in the spring of 1990, the Athabasca Glacier is 6 kilometers long, average 1 kilometer in width, and the thickness of its ice layer is 300 meters—it equals the height of the Eiffel Tower. In surface, its current velocity is approximately 25 meters every year. However, because of the greenhouse effect, its stealthy walking speed cannot match the melting speed.

Using the Athabasca Glacier water to boil Fenghua County's minnows can make one fully enjoy the intimate harmony between fish and water. In addition, like the upstream-going minnows from the Fenghua County of China, the quietly extended Athabasca Glacier has firm and unyielding will —

I am afraid it's too late to enter you,
Everyday I get impatient,
Everyday I become feeble and retreating
More impatiently than impatient ...

With an expectation of three-million years ago
My desire has swelled and extended in dark —
I move to you in silence
Matchlessly hard and firm in surface,

Deep inside,
Adhesively, turbulent desire arises,
I thirst to touch your gentle grassland,
Enter into your roaring lake.

Ingredients

Bacon, garlic salt, sausage, red cherries, lettuce, chili powder.

Method

1) Quickly boil bacon strips. Scoop up from the water and dry them.
2) Spread out the bacon and add some garlic salt.
3) Wrap each sausage with a slice of bacon. Roll up and fix the rolls with toothpicks.
4) Put aluminum foil on the bottom and bake the rolls for eight to ten minutes.
5) When serving, first decorate the plate with lettuce and red cherries.

Note

Dishes for the purpose of male potency can easily cause indigestion. Therefore, be careful not to indulge. For example, if this dish is over-consumed, every five seconds one will produce a seven-second fart.

Illustration

The utmost sex appeal lies in preparation; the preparation of this dish is full of the spirit of sculpturing. When wrapping sausages with bacon strips, pay particular attention to geographical locations — target sausage at the middle of bacon, carefully roll up and adjust. Be especially aware that that sausage cannot be inclined to the left; only by being technically unbiased can one stay impartial and appropriate so as to bring into play the national spirit of utmost grandness, firmness, impartialness, and righteousness.

This dish emphasizes the spiritual. Remain in an unhurried manner when cooking. Be steadfast, prudent, spiritual, commanding, focused, and single-minded...so as to achieve the goal of using the strong to attack the weak. The entanglement of the two kinds of meat is similar to flesh between two sexes. The encountering of two sexes is similar to the confrontation of two armies. According to Master Chiang of the World Impartiality Studies, "Before all actions, one must first stay still, and then stay calm. By doing so, safety may be achieved." Prior to action, if one can first remain still, calm, and tranquil, then he will be unshakable and influenced by nothing outside.

If the sense of taste unexpectedly sleeps
Unawake even being shaken, if the tongue
Is content to retain sovereignty over a small corner,
please use
Chili powder to sculpture my taste bud, like
High heat sculptures hot oil,
Hot oil sculptures smell,
Smell sculptures carnal desire,
Love is awakened in carnal desire —

Inside the love-baked flesh
Lives a bat,
Gazes from the depth of hole,
flying, a flock of bats
A flock of hungry bats
From inside the repressive hole
Unfold in a large scale —

Like the wind unfolding your
Texture of life,
Emotional chili powder, revealing
Inside wrapped
Oath. Between lips
The dialogue of the flesh unfolds,
My body is wrapping
Another warm and fragrant body,
Inside my eyes
Another pair of eyes.

RETURN MY COUNTRYLAND*

Ingredients

Tapioca rice, hard sugar, coconut milk, milk, ice cubes, an egg, Kiwi fruit, blue syrup.

Method

1) Boil Tapioca rice: after water boils, put in Tapioca rice, stir while cooking to make Tapioca rice transparent. When boiling again, add a bowl of cold water, repeat three times. Remove from the stove. Use cold water to

---

* A patriotic slogan of Yueh Fei (1103–1141), one of China's most honorable generals in the Sung dynasty (960–1279). In the early twelfth century, the Jurchen invaded China. The Sung lost the North and retreated to the South and designated Hangchou of Chekiang Province as its "temporary capital." The Southern Sung was eager to reach a peace agreement with the Jurchen, but one of its generals, Yueh Fei, opposed the peace deal and vowed to force the Jurchen to "return my countryland." He was imprisoned and died in 1141. The slogan was adopted by the Nationalist Government to express its determination in taking back the mainland.

cool off the cooked Tapioca rice. After filtering, add some ice water to keep its wetness.

2) Mix hard sugar with water, cook until melted. Then, add coconut milk and milk. Turn off the gas. After cooling down, add Tapioca rice.

3) Use juicer to smash ice cubes, and then lay them on top of Tapioca rice juice.

4) Add blue syrup on the edge of plate.

5) Put a fresh egg yolk on crushed ice. Chop Kiwi into small cubes, and then decorate around the yolk.

Illustration

When yolk meets ice, it congeals. The scenery is as magnificent as the sunset at dusk. The yolk is surrounded by blue syrup, which makes yolk and the Kiwi look like an island floating in the ocean. The island makes one think of the mainland.

The red begonia, only closing my eyes
Can I see your wheat-colored skin,
Your breasts, graceful

Hills and plain, your
Crotch, forests and rivers,
Like an ice-cube, those disappearing
Years of the fruit,

Close to me with stifling fragrance,
Your congestive form, I imagine
Erection, makes me arrhythmic
Mountain peaks, keep rising,
When my hands move close to the pulsating terrain,
There are rainy snow and winter thunder. I thirst for

Touching your territory once again,
Breathing on your body, I thirst for
Reentering your body, working and crying,
Like lush raindrops and seeds
Return to childhood home.

Dusk falls on eyes,
My longing is like an island
The surrounding waves, unwilling to rest,
Forever ruminating
The taste of kissing and embracing.

CAVERN IN PARADISE

Ingredients

Taros, sweet potato powder, sugar, hard sugar, green beans, sweet red beans, Lima beans.

Method

1) Peel taros, then chop into small cubes. Steam and mash taro cubes when hot.
2) Mix mashed taros with sweet potato powder and sugar, then roll them into a round ball. Cut it into small pieces, and carefully knead them in round shape.
3) Mix hard sugar with water and boil for future use.
4) Boil half pot of water, and put in taro balls. When boiling, add cold water. When boiling again, add cold water. Add more cold water after boiling until balls float on water. Scoop up balls and put them in a bowl. Add hard sugar water to serve.

Note

The sense of tasting is the top priority in making taro balls. If one feels that the combination of taros and sweet potatoes is a little drab, add sweet red beans, lima beans, and green beans to complicate the feeling of chewing.

Illustration

Our love is like taro balls —
Mashed taros and sweet potato powder must elimi-
       nate
Individual differences, only so
My mud contains you,
Your powder contains me. We

Make love in high heat,
Yet avoid getting entangled, in
Harsh years, impulse
floats, then gets irritated
Sinking, hopelessly falling
Into the burning hot abyss. We

Need kisses deeper than the abyss
To communicate our unforgettable sugar content. We

Unite like a sauna,
Cool down quickly, then continue
To heat up, twirling in dense fog,
You breathe in my bosom
Seize the chance before firewood burns to ashes
Dance one more graceful waltz
Melt scars into a smile, fusing
The tasty feelings of grief and joy.

DRAGON FROM THE NORTH SEA

Ingredients

Prawn, butter, lemon, pepper powder, garlic salt.

Method

1) Trim off the pointed thorns on prawn's head as well as the big feet on the chest, peel off the body's shell, but keep the shell on head and tail. Get rid of the muddy intestines, wash prawn clean, and make it dry.
2) Heat up butter in a pan, put in prawn, and fry with gentle heat.
3) When prawn's body becomes red, turn over and fry the other side, add lemon juice.
4) When it is about done, spread garlic salt and pepper powder.
5) When the juicy sauce is about to dry, ladle the cooked prawn from the pan.

Note

When cooking the prawn, one should not trim off the pointed part on prawn's tail, because this part nourishes kidneys and solidifies sperm. Otherwise male gourmets will fear castration.

Illustration

Peel off the outside shell, clean the body filth,
Shyly and nakedly reveals
Manly self-esteem,
Retreat. Erection. Retreat. Erection.
Like a wriggling prawn, earnestly
Maintains a posture of leaping,
The body obscenely assailed by fire
Reddens esteem,
The Titanic-like pointed tail
Waves and surges in butter...

The swelling effect is the key.
Provided reuniting with the exhilarating hot pan,
        that pointed tail
Provided colliding with your burning eyes
All colors turn dissipated simultaneously,

Colors turn into fragrance, fragrance transforms
        into fire,
The exultation is like
Insatiable rosy clouds. Hyperemia
Is an aesthetic tool,
An expression of an iron man,
That pointed tail, because of hyperemia
Is more beautiful than a beauty's brain,
Harder than the head of an iron man.

FIERCE TIGER FROM THE SOUTH MOUNTAIN

Ingredients

1 Bangladesh Tiger penis, 2 preserved plums, 4 leaves of purple mint, 1 piece of seasoned seaweed, 2 bowls of rice, and a little red wine.

Method

1) Quickly rinse and dry rice.
2) Put rice into electric cooker; add tiger penis, plums, seaweed, water, and red wine.
3) Braise rice for another ten minutes after it's done.
4) Take out tiger penis and rub it clean. Put in a safe place for future use. Also take out plum seeds and seaweeds. Mix rice and plums evenly.
5) Chop up purple mint leaves and wrap them in cloth. Wash it clean and squeeze out water. Sprinkle it on rice.

Note

The Taiwanese men's physique is not suitable for eating tiger penis. Thus, it is recommended that they should go to a Chinese medicine store to buy a plastic one for substitution.

Illustration

Like love-making, routinized cooking is similar to using a ruler to paint. It lacks not only courage but also imagination.

The key to the success of cooking rice lies in the amount of water. A slight difference in the amount of water will seriously affect the taste. When cooking, be attentive that the moisture and quality of rice should be in harmony with the day's weather and temperature and adjust water and heat accordingly.

In addition, the qualities of water and rice should be emphasized. Avoid using lead poisoned rice or chemical-polluted rice as well as the tap water with a high chlorine content.

In order to make a pot of tasty rice, one needs to first understand the nature of rice. Only by doing so one can tease out the delicacy of rice. Speed is the key: first get rid of the dirty stuff among grains of rice. But the speed of rice-rinsing and water-pouring must be quick, because the smell of rice bran melted out in water may be easily absorbed by thirsty grains of rice. Although quickness is required, avoid rudeness. The washing and rinsing action must be gentle and tender. Change water repeatedly until it becomes clear.

Since ancient times, most heroes have kidney dysfunctions. Tiger penis protects Chinese men's esteem. It startles the universe and moves the gods. Taiwan is the largest production base of tiger penis in the world. Although fewer than 1,000 tigers exist in today's world, there are still more than 30,000 tiger penises in the Taiwan market.

Fear is the only thing left.
Relying on fear, they unceasingly
Reproduce and reproduce long penises,
Nakedly worshipped
By fear. Today

I am a tiger,
Waiting for you on the steep cliff,
Determined despite of the frost, the dew, and the
dark night, waiting and waiting,
Escape from hungry hunting rifles,
flashlights, escape from
Rumors. Intentionally I fall into
Your hidden trap, leave
Memorable scars

Moonlight deploys guards in the wilderness,
Cold wind goes on patrol,
I am still tenderly waiting for you,
My obsession is like sharp teeth,
Extends in a thundering rage,
Tears off your ornaments,
Bites your neck. My claws are
Uncontrollable fire,
Imitate leaping and jumping, attacking
Your breasts,
Your round ass.

*SPIRITUAL REFORM**

Ingredients

Female crab, white wine, young ginger, lemon, tangerine, and honey.

Method

1) Use a toothbrush to carefully bath the crab.
2) Use a syringe to inject white wine into her, untie her, and examine her misty eyes and drunken manner with a smile.
3) Pour water into the steamer, boil. Put the crab in the steamer, belly up.
4) Cook for about 8 minutes over high heat.
5) Cook with dipped sauce: honey, young ginger powder, lemon, and tangerine juice.

---

*   "Spiritual Reform" is a political slogan promoted by Taiwanese President Lee Teng-hui after he was officially elected by the people of Taiwan. It is intended to raise the awareness of the importance of culture and to improve the quality of life in the industrialized society of Taiwan.

Illustration

Flesh must be fresh in order to have a lively spirit.
Facing a fresh crab, one feels like possessing a lively
spirit. With a lively spirit, one must also have a lively
body. To replace granulated sugar with honey and
to replace vinegar with lemon juice is a kind of spiritual reform, effective in seducing fresh bodies. All
reforms must start with the salvation of the root,
because

The sense of delicate taste, like lustful desires, arises
Between eyes
Not between legs. Your eyes
Are a pair of wings,
Helping me fly, helping me to
fly over the ocean,
Over spring, over the body's
Equator. When I

Hold you with both hands,
Spread out your limbs,
Strip off your clothes, as if
A pregnant lover's reliance,
Every inch of flesh is a song,

Searching for my soul, as if a
Dried-up river valley desires
To embrace and kiss water. As if

You are a beautiful crab, drunk and
Waiting for my skillful hands as a cooking artist
To take care of you. You wait in a nap
For my gourmet's tongue
To taste you.

BE PATIENT, NO RUSH*

Ingredients

1 black bone cock, 5cc King Kong liquor, 1 big old ginger, 4 green onions, 1 glass of rice wine.

Method

1) Better effect will be achieved if both the bone and the flesh of the selected cock appear black. When selecting, one may examine cock's tongue. If it looks black, then that is the right one.
2) No hurry to kill the cock. Before killing, pour 5cc King Kong liquor into the cock. Bleed the cock half an hour later.
3) No hurry to cook the cock. After bleeding and before cooking, give the cock a massage.
4) No hurry to heat up. The water level inside

---

* `"Be Patient, No Rush" is also a political slogan promoted by Taiwanese President Lee Teng-hui in the 1990s, aiming to "properly" deal with mainland China's economic and political intricacies.

the pot should just submerge the cock. Put a big piece of old ginger into the pot. When boiling, add 4 green onions and 1 cup of rice wine, then put the naked cock in and cover the pot.

5) No hurry to take the lid off. Let water boil for five more minutes. Turn off the heat. Take the lid off after residual heat cools down.

6) No hurry to open one's mouth. When serving, apply a layer of salt to the cock's body based on individual taste.

7) No hurry to stick out one's tongue. Chop the cock into pieces and add sesame oil and chopped green onion.

Illustration

It is unavoidable that the cock being castrated is full of anger and fear. All anger and fear will be stored inside the cock's flesh. According to the principle of the food chain, animals' emotion before execution will affect peoples' feeling. If too many depressed animal corpses are consumed, over a long period, it will accumulatively make *yang* elements weaker and eventually lead to kidney dysfunctions.

The King Kong liquor produced by the Kimmen Winery is imbued with the memory of the August 23rd Artillery War* and has absorbed the marrows of all kinds of huge cannons. Thus, the liquor is particularly powerful. Together with the great result of massage, King Kong liquor can not only soothe the cock's emotion and make its flesh relaxed, but also uplift the cock's appearance.

But King Kong liquor cannot be overused. Otherwise, it will bring serious physical changes to that cock—all cock feathers will erect. Firm and lasting, the erected feathers are very hard to remove.

Be attentive that, when making this dish, one's manner must be refined: as if trying to cover up a misdeed but to make it more conspicuous; as if try-

* In September 1954, after a series of statements by mainland China promising to "liberate" Taiwan, Communist forces launched an artillery bombardment of Kimmen, the largest of the offshore islands held by the Nationalists. On August 23, 1958, the second round of bombardment, considered by many as the most severe, began with forces of mainland China firing on Kimmen, which triggered another Offshore Island Crisis.

ing to refuse the temptation but actually to embrace
it. Use one's concealing art of cooking to express
the mixed flavor of joy and fear —

If you make me drunk and deadly immortal
I will make you stuffed and lustily dizzy

You breathe deeply
I supply you with fragrance

"You widely open your mouth
I keep it stuffed"

You massage me
I give you temptation

You burn me with your hungry eyes
I submerge you with greedy drooling

Ah Ah Ah, you give me heat
I am eager to be trampled

THREE-INCH GOLDEN LOTUS

Ingredients

2 *jin** slim and graceful pig feet, 200 gram glossy garlic heads, 1 bottle of coke, ½ bowl of soy sauce, some Chinese anises and peppers.

Method

1) Wash pig feet carefully, remove foot hair, cut into pieces, and dry them with tissue papers.
2) Use boiling water to get rid of the stinking smell of the pig feet, scoop them up from boiling water, and clean the boiled pieces.
3) Use coke and soy sauce to boil pig feet, add garlic heads and Chinese anises, then simmer until well cooked.
4) Decorate plate with green vegetables before serving.

* A Chinese unit of weight. One *jin* or catty equals ½ kilogram.

Illustration

Slenderness is the principle in selecting pig feet. It should be emphasized that the pig feet's proportion must be well balanced beginning from the thigh, the line should gracefully turn inward until without edges and corners. Second, ankles should be thin and slim, but reveal no bones. In addition, the selected feet must have intelligence.

A small and intelligent foot can effectively arouse the body, triggering positive physical responses. According to Ling Hsuan's *Unofficial Biography of Chao Fei-yen*, "Emperor Ch'en of Han used to go hunting in the early morning and got sick in snow. He became weak and could not achieve erection. But whenever he held Chao-i's feet, his sexual desire was aroused and his male organ erected at that instant."

A pair of well-cooked feet is full of allurement, as elegant as a lover's feet.

Adding to the above is the fact that the delight of enjoying the "Three-Inch Lotus" differs between day and night. As Li Yu pointed out in his *A Temporary*

Lodge for My Leisure Thoughts: "Slim as if shapeless, the more one looks, the more pitiful one feels. This applies to the daytime situation. Soft as if boneless, the more one cherishes, the longer one wants to touch. This describes the nighttime situation."

First place green vegetables on the snow-white porcelain plate, then arrange the elegant feet in order—to put the graceful feet on jade green bed of vegetables is not only for decoration, but also a bashful form of expression. It satisfies one's voyeurism and stimulates one's appetite.

At a teeth-itchy night
One is driven by impulse to bite
There is an image
Manifesting itself with hungry curves
As if in the middle of a bed
Inviting a voyeur's eyes

Their eyes carry fire
Neurotically
Burning her whole body with a gaze

Her shadow hides
Inside a strip of swinging foot-binding cloth
Exquisitely unfolds beautiful images
Sometimes fluctuating like a collective cough
Sometimes looking like an exclamation mark in
     history

RED APRICOTS REACH OUT OF THE WALL

Ingredients

1 newly unearthed dinosaur egg, 8 *liang**** chicken testes, 6 *liang* quail eggs, 1 *jin* spareribs, ½ *jin* taros, ½ of a Chinese cabbage, 4 *liang* red jujubes, 4 *liang* peanuts, 4 *qian***** Chinese cinnamons, 4 *liang* chestnuts, 4 *liang* shark skin, 3 sea cucumbers, 1 bowl of shark's fins, 4 *liang* skinless garlic heads, 2 bowls of soup-stock, 3 bowls of olive oil, ½ bowl of flour.

Method

1) Wash sturdy taros clean, cut into pieces;
   Rinse fishy shark's fins for future use;
   Wash fishy sharkskin and sea cucumbers clean, cut into segments;
   Wash clean and dry mighty testes;
   Wash snow-white Chinese cabbage clean, cut into segments;

*   A Chinese unit of weight. One *liang* equals 50 grams.
** A Chinese unit of weight. One *qian* equals 5 grams.

Rinse plump chestnuts, then steep to soften
    them;
Rinse and dry juicy ribs.

2) Hot and restless olive oil is waiting in the pan,
    Waiting for taros, and floured ribs, one af-
      ter another
    Entering, until the outer surface
    Turned yellow.

    A jar,
    A jar opens its mouth
    Embracing taros and ribs,
    Embracing garlic-fried cabbage,
    Embracing dinosaur egg, quail eggs, and tes-
      tes,
    Embracing red jujubes, peanuts, cinna-
      mons, and chestnuts,
    Embracing shark's fins and sea cucumbers,
      embracing sharkskin.
    Add water into soup-stock to submerge the
      materials, mix with salt.

Cover the full and swelling jar with plastic wrap,
and then put it inside a steamer and steam for two
hours.

Note

Farmers from China's Henan Province should in no circumstance eat dinosaur eggs.

Illustration

Ancient wisdom teaches us: eating liver nourishes liver, eating brain nourishes brain, eating egg nourishes egg. Relying on their gigantic figures, the dinosaur and its eggs have bewitched human minds for thousands of years. Big is beautiful, a hint of wisdom, and a metaphor of power. The newly unearthed dinosaur eggs have magic effect on fertility. Women who do not want kids must in no circumstance try them.

Next to water, steam all kinds of cooked leftovers, make rich flavors out of the essence of poverty —

I thirst for your entry,
Inside the deep pan as solid as culture,
Inside that jar as heavily protected as a household,
All kinds of coldly treated odors:
Local chicken testes,

Taros from the south,
Cabbage from the north,
Shark's fins and sea cucumbers from ocean,
And red jujubes, peanuts, cinnamons, chestnuts,
As well as the quail eggs recoiling at the corner,
Huddle together to exchange the body temperature,
Like southern accents and northern tunes, hugging
Inside a boiling hot spring,
Different skin colors ironing out the same
Feelings. Our bodies and juices
Twine together, sentimental, at last, melting into
Mutual flavors.

RAINCLOUDS OVER THE WU MOUNTAIN

Ingredients

Fuji apple from Japan, black sugar, butter, cassia
powder

Method

1) Select a Fuji apple as majestic as the outer
   shape of Fuji mountain, wash and clean it.
2) Use a seeder to remove the seeds along the
   downward direction of the apple's stem.
3) Make seasoning sauce: 1 apple with approximately 10 gram black sugar, 1 teaspoon butter, plus some cassia powder.
4) Mix seasoning sauce, pour it into the apple.
5) Use toothpicks to make holes on the skin of
   the apple, place it into the 190 degrees cen-
   tigrade preheated oven, bake for 40 minutes.

Illustration

Spring breeze blows and ripens apples,
The tempting crimson shines,
Baked and reddened
The impulse of licking.

The development of lust is like baking apples,
No stem, no seeds,
Only colors with deep fragrance
Dizzily spreading from the mature chest,
Like powdering Fuji mountain at sunset
In the crimson of the first night, tingling
Embracing and rejecting the tears of the lost love.

The color passes through the eyes,
Then stays, my body
Is wetted
By your erotic look. But
My eyes are a storage room
For holy utensils, collecting
Solemn love rituals, and
Inexhaustible holy water.

Our love is
Like the baked apple, internally it
Requires just a little sugar
But no lack of sweetness; on the surface
flow the happy tears, which are
Like fragrant milk
Nurturing the imperfect world.

PASSION RIPPLES IN SPRING

Ingredients

Dried roses, ginger sugar, common cnidium fruits, and mountain water.

Method

1) After spring water boils, stuff common cnidium fruits into a medicine bag.
2) Simmer common cnidium fruits over medium heat, then add spring water. Bring it to boil three times.
3) Put in ginger sugar until it melts.
4) Filter common cnidium fruits, and spread dry roses when removing from heat.

Illustration

"Passion Ripples in Spring" is the best honeymoon drink during Spring. Perhaps in a strange corner on earth, you check in at a hotel before sunset. After drawing the curtain aside and unzipping, you would feel a sense of remoteness, aimless wandering, and dreamlike life emanate from your chest and belly. At this time, drink a cup of "Passion Ripples in Spring." The dreamy fragrance will spread inside your body.

In order to improve the effectiveness, please recite Chang Ts'o's "Love Poems of Tea" before drinking.

This cup of tea only serves as an appetizer, but what it brings is raging lust. Those who suffer from strong *yang* and weak *yin* must abstain from over-drinking. Avoid anxiousness. When dropped into boiling water, dry roses will immediately stretch and swell —

You are the dry rose,
I am the boiling water, embracing you;

I moisten you,
You enter me —

"Let your soft dryness
Unfold inside me, spreading;"

You faintly open up within me,
I gently moan without —

"Let my moisture
Smooth your looks."

Let my softness and your hardness
Produce rosy feelings,

Let my moistness and your dryness
Become a fragrant vortex in an embrace.

Ingredients

¼ teaspoon *emu* eggshell, ½ *jin* squid paste, 6 salted yolks, 2 pieces of seasoned seaweeds, 2 cups of almond slices, lettuce, lemon slices, moth orchid.

Method

1) Grind *emu* eggshell into powder.
2) Divide squid paste into 6 equal shares. Add *emu* eggshell powder and mix thoroughly, and then place the shares on oiled glassine.
3) Cut each seaweed into four pieces. Use each piece to wrap a raw salted yolk and then wrap it again with squid paste. Then, paste up almond slices evenly, like embedding beads* together.

---

* An allusion to the Ch'en Chin-hsing Incident of 1998. Ch'en became a fugitive after he kidnapped, tortured, raped, and eventually killed the daughter of a famous Taiwanese actress. While on the run, he committed several other rape crimes. After he was caught, Taiwan's tabloid magazines reported that Ch'en embedded beads around his penis to "enhance" his sexual power.

4) Fry squid balls in oil over gentle heat until they turn golden. Scoop up from oil and let them drain. Cut each ball in half and arrange them on lettuce, and then decorate with moth orchid and lemon slices.

5) Add a few drops of lemon juice before eating. Dewdrops accelerate the blossom of peony. But avoid excessive drops. Otherwise the tart flavor will irritate one with heartache.

Note

Aboriginal Australians must not eat *emu* eggshell powder.

Illustration

Like feudal morality, squid paste locks tightly and deeply, continuing to torture. With difficulty, youthful vigor struggles to break out of the encirclement. The two opposite forces, therefore, spark the flavor of complication.

The half cut squid balls look like a bright moon, like a pair of pupils staring back. Decorated by petals and lemon, they can build up an eating environment described in the poetic line "When a flower's shadow stirred and brushed the wall,/For a moment I thought it the shadow of a lover coming."*

Like a bright moon,
Illuminated by a kind of heat?
Lemons pair to spread fragrance,
Moth orchids in couples
Swing tender pistils,
Facing the dark side of lake and mountain,
The bright moon turns her face from the mountain rift —

Witnessing a kind of vigor, wrapped up
Inside the soft and warm body,
Layer after layer, the fleshy bud
Waiting for full blossom.

Ah there is a kind of warmth and fragrance, half refusing, half inviting
Unbuttoned from round fissure,
Seducing lips to get closer,
Seducing the tongue to launch an adventure.

* The two lines are quoted from the T'ang (617–906) writer Yuan Chen's "The Story of Ts'ui Ying-ying."

SECRET RENDEZVOUS

Ingredients

1 male goose in high heat, 20cc xo brandy, 2 old
gingers, 6 green onions, bottle of Shaohsin wine,
Chinese basil, soybean sauce, young ginger, orange
juice, honey.

Method

1) First starve the goose for 49 hours and then
   feed him with top class xo brandy. When
   his drunken eyes become hazy, proceed with
   the bleeding and pluck his feathers.
2) Pour clean water into a deep pot. Water level
   must be over the whole body of the goose.
   Add two pieces of old ginger and cook over
   high heat.
3) When boiling, add green onion, Shaohsin
   wine, and the naked goose. Cover the pot
   and simmer for 20 minutes. Then turn off
   heat.
4) After the cooked goose cools down, cut him
   into pieces. Dip in sauce when eating.

5) Sauce ingredients: soybean sauce, young ginger powder, orange juice, honey, and Chinese basil.

Illustration

Keep goose soaked inside the pot until it cools down, because the key emphasis is on the texture and the feel of the goose. To take good care of the skin not only requires outside coating but also demands inside moistening.

The posture of this goose is of vital importance. The original posture must be retained after he is cut into pieces. As for the layout, consult Leonardo da Vinci's painting "Leda and the Swan."

Be sure not to pick up the knife, fork, and chopsticks in a hurry after the dish is served on the table. First stare at the goose and then carefully examine the goose with deep passion.

In calm and fragrant water,
That naked goose shyly
Smiles. Even losing his footing,

Falls into water, that sound is pleasing to the ear
Like a full moon's smile.
When our eyes meet,
Inside my body
Is there anything I cannot open up for you?

The crooked goose head acts like kissing,
The strong right wing spreads as if to embrace,
Surrounding the neck, the trace of the love-bite is like
A silk ribbon of lightning. His breast, his shoulder
Occupy my chastity, my belief.
Swallow me, his erotic mouth,
Touches me, his black webfoot.

As if there is wind blowing, one can hear
Huge wings slap leaves, an agitated
Raining sound, wind breathing in rifts of trees,
As if hugging, in trembling
They gradually return to silence, the fragrant flower of
        music
Blooms on lips.

MANDARIN DUCKS IN ONE NIGHT STAND

Ingredients

Tilapia fish, fermented bean curd, homemade fragrant fruit wine, fragrant fruit juice, ginger powder, pepper powder, chopped green onion.

Method

1) Wash and clean the Tilapia fish.
2) Grind ginger into powder. Cut pepper and green onion for future use.
3) Add water to fermented bean curd, fragrant fruit wine and juice, and ginger powder, and then mix thoroughly. Boil the mix in a pot.
4) Put in the Tilapia fish and pepper powder. Spread chopped green onion when it's about to be done.

Note

Eating fish depends on opportunities, and being full depends on wisdom. Be sure to wipe oil away from your mouth after finishing the course. If one is not careful enough and suffers from overeating, please follow the example of Chu I-tsun:* "Take a leisurely walk, use hands to rub face, ribs, and belly, and face upward to take four or five deep breaths" so as to avoid food-poisoning.

Illustration

To transform the rot into wonders and the ordinary into nobility is the basic spirit for enhancing the male potency. The reason why fresh Tilapia is so cheap is probably due to its muddy flavor. The way to improve this is to introduce fermented bean curd and fragrant fruit. Use fermented bean curd to get rid of the muddy flavor, and then use fragrant fruit wine and juice to tease out the fish's deliciousness.

It is a must to catch Tilapia in a pair. Fragrant fruit wine must be covertly and privately brewed. Once sold in public, it will lose the intriguing flavor of a clandestine affair. In addition, this course is not appropriate to be listed in the menu of a public ban-

---

* Chu I-tsun (1629–1709), a Chinese poet and historian in the Ch'ing dynasty (1644–1911).

quet. It is only good for individual enjoyment when
one feels lonely late at night.

This is the situation,
Furtively
In the raging flame, it is impossible to turn back,
Everything ripens at fast speed. There is a feeling
of sourness, bitterness, and sweetness
Tangled together in carnal desire,
That fills the oil pan
Struggling, wriggling,
Stirred and fried time and again, ah,
There is torture like a lovesickness,
That one tastes only alone;

There is a color,
That never really arrives, only
Drifts over thought, like a person's shadow
Passing through a dream,
In a silent winter night, ah
There is an experience,
Regardless of joy or bitter,
I only care about
Sharing the taste of life.

CARRY ON THE FAMILY NAMES

Ingredients

2 pork tripe (with spermatic duct), 2 *qian* Tuckahoe, 2 *qian* Chinese Angelica Root, 2 *qian* Prepared
Rehmannia Root, 1 *qian* fried White Peony Root, 1
qian Ch'uanhsiung Rhizome, 1 *qian* Gordon Euryale
Seed, rice wine.

Method

> Wash and clean the pork tripe, cut into large
> slices, throw into boiling water, and burn
> away the foul smell.
> Throw 5 bowls of clean water into the bo-
> som of the pot,
> Throw all ingredients into the bosom of the
> pot,
> Ch'uanhsiung Rhizome rubs the pork tripe
> Gordon Euryale Seed coquettes with Tucka-
> hoe
> Rehmannia Root and Angelica Root concert
> in an up-and-down motion
> Until after about an hour,

Clear water has transformed into holy syrup
that nourishes the kidneys and sperm,
Pork tripe has ripened and softened, as fragrant as
A cotton-padded mattress.

Illustration

Throw un-boiled pork into the cooking pot, just like
A marriage without the baptism of love,
The carnal desire must be simmered by increasing
    incense,
Restraining the explosive impulse.

Under control as long as a marriage,
Boiling water passionately plays
The mating music of the spermatic duct,
Using the mask of morality
It unceasingly conceals a primitive interest.

Simmering is a kind of traditional rhythm,
The willow grows along the lotus pond,
Water vapor in deep valleys turns to mountain mist,
Peaches and plums silently spread fragrance along
    the spring creek.

Ah, let us compose together a song with shape,
      color, and meaning,
Shape breeds color,
Warmth reproduces fragrance,
Yin and Yang battles against each other,
Water and fire celebrate together.

MALE POTENCY REGAINED

Ingredients

1 drake just in oestrus, 1 bottle of Taiwan beer, 10 *qian* Chinese caterpillar fungus, 6 slices old ginger, 1 bowl of membraneless garlic, 1 bowl of soy sauce, 2 red peppers, 6 green onions, some crystal sugar and old Matsu wine.

Method

1) First soak the drake with old Matsu wine.
2) Once the drake is clean, put garlic, old ginger, and Chinese caterpillar fungus inside the drake's belly.
3) Place the drake, Taiwan beer, soy sauce, crystal sugar, red pepper, and green onion in a pan. Cook with high heat. When boiling, reduce to a simmer.
4) Turn every 10 minutes. After about 40 minutes, evaporate the sauce over medium heat.
5) The remaining juicy sauce can be used as dip when serving.

Note

If sliced into thin pieces, drake meat can serve as snacks. If one carries the drake meat with him, he can enhance his potency anytime he wants. However, the most effective use of this dish requires nine right occasions if tasted on palms, shoulders, swing boards, and in quilt, under the lamp, in snow, under curtain or screen or bamboo fence, it will produce the best results.

Illustration

It is a must to select a drake just in oestrus but with no mating experience. Massage him after soaked in wine. Then, remove the thick fat to allow the fragrance to spread completely.

Surplus fat is like
Overflowing promises, like
Food with excessive monosodium glutamate,
Sweet caresses in an inattentive manner.

When promise nakedly
Bathes in the deep pan with an overflow of rhythm
Every inch of skin can be
Simmered into music through a tipsy feeling,
Fragrant and sweet nocturne.

That expression of your eye is my string,
That muscular solid body
In the dream with flicking candlelight is impromptu
Like Jazz inside me
Twisting back and forth.

Ah, we are all musical notes in this world,
Destined in the deep pan of time
Ensemble and ensemble, you and I
Match well with each other,
Murmur at oneself yet
Gaze at each other, orchestrating
Joyful or sorrowful themes.

Ingredients

Squid, Chinese chives, pepper, ginger, pepper powder, sesame oil.

Method

1) Wash the squid clean and chop them into
   long pieces.
2) Wash the Chinese chives clean and chop
   them into segments; cut ginger into shreds
   and ground the pepper into powder.
3) When the oiled pan turns hot, slightly stir-
   fry pepper and ginger, then add the squid.
4) Add the Chinese chives, pepper powder,
   sesame oil, salt, and then stir-fry evenly.

Illustration

First, use old ginger to rub the bottom of the pan so
that a pleasant lubricating effect can be produced
when the squid and Chinese chives are added. Only
by using such a heart-touching pan can the dreamy,

romantic, imaginative, and licentious taste be produced.

That raging flame, unceasingly tantalizes me,
In the kitchen filled with desires,
All imagination is inside
A hot and lubricating pan, all
Materials, imbued with sexual implications —

It gets up often in dreamy midnights, extends
Its paws and teeth, playing with my cheek, arousing
My worship, my fear: potency
Is not a sickly weak noun, but
A huge, calligraphy-like
Transitive verb, a cruel
Modal verb, full of milky flavor,
Breeding sound and color, association
Vigorous images, rich in
Elasticity, changes. It is evil

Like the sexy vocabulary of the *fin-de-siècle*,
As if intercourse between fire and water
Fucked the noun, that indecent noun,
Fucked the adjective, that licentious adjective,
Like grammars with weird sentence patterns,
Fucked the verb that stimulated the verb. It is

As uproarious as the cooking pan,
Moaning and singing
Boiling songs;
It is sly, like wind
flirting with willow leaves, flirting with peonies
Like a lover's tongue, warming up
Stiff language.
It is a reptile,
The odorous snake crawls
Out of the hole of ideas.

AN ERECT PILLAR

Ingredients

1 long banana, 2 large AA eggs, 2 teaspoons tiger head honey from the Tapachien Mountain, 6 full teaspoons soybean powder, 1 full teaspoon wine.

Method

1) Mix soybean powder, eggs, and wine together, stir evenly, and make the mix into a thick and fishy paste.
2) Fully soak the skinless and erected banana in the mix. Make sure the firm banana is fully soaked with the fishy paste.
3) Use hot oil to fry the banana until it turns golden. Dip into tiger head honey when served.

Illustration

Honey must be made out of the tiger head bees from the Tapachien Mountain. Accompanied by the flowing and decadent symphony of the Madala

Creek, the tiger head bees boldly drive on against the severe gale of high elevation and shuttle in and out of the deep forest of thick and straight pines. Their honey conveys the sublime secret of deep mountains.

The contour of the selected banana should be straight, not crooked. Try one's best to pick an upright one. Strive for its hardness and elasticity and avoid dejectedness. Only with adequate hardness and elasticity can it strive forth in the torment of heat —

That is the magic of shape and esteem.
On the verge of sinking,
The magician uses both hard and soft tactics,
Pulls out a ruler from the arched door,
Measures the size,
Throws it to the sky —

Turns it longer and longer
Transforms it into the Tokyo Tower;

Turns askew and askew
Transforms it into the Leaning Tower of Pisa.

The magician uses hallucination,
Uplifting and uplifting
Uplifts the Monument of National Heroes;

Erecting and erecting
Erects the totem of the male.

GREEN INTEGER
Pataphysics and Pedantry

Edited by Per Bregne
Douglas Messerli, *Publisher*

Essays, Manifestos, Statements, Speeches, Maxims,
Epistles, Diaristic Notes, Narratives, Natural Histories,
Poems, Plays, Performances, Ramblings, Revelations
and all such ephemera as may appear necessary
to bring society into a slight tremolo of confusion
and fright at least.

*

Green Integer Books